This Book Belongs to:

Follow Southeast Asian Archaeology on Instagram! Take a picture of your finished pages and tag **@southeastasianarchaeology** to get featured. Learn more about the archaeology of Southeast Asia at **www.SoutheastAsianArchaeology.com**

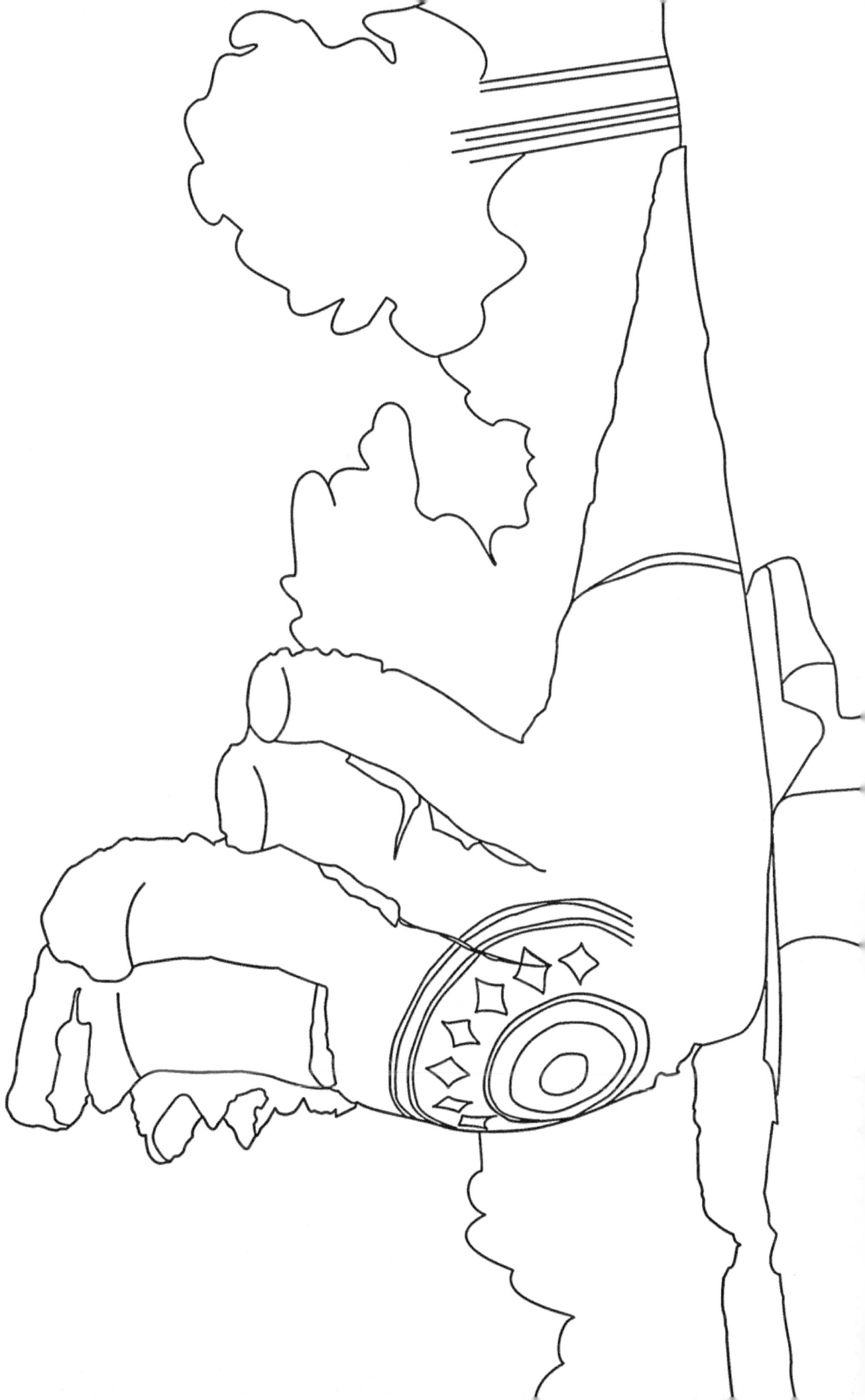

The 9th century temple of Bakong in the Roluos group of temples at Angkor, Cambodia, features the first instance of bridges in the form of a naga or serpent deity. This early form of the naga bridge rests on the ground, while later versions are set on balustrades.

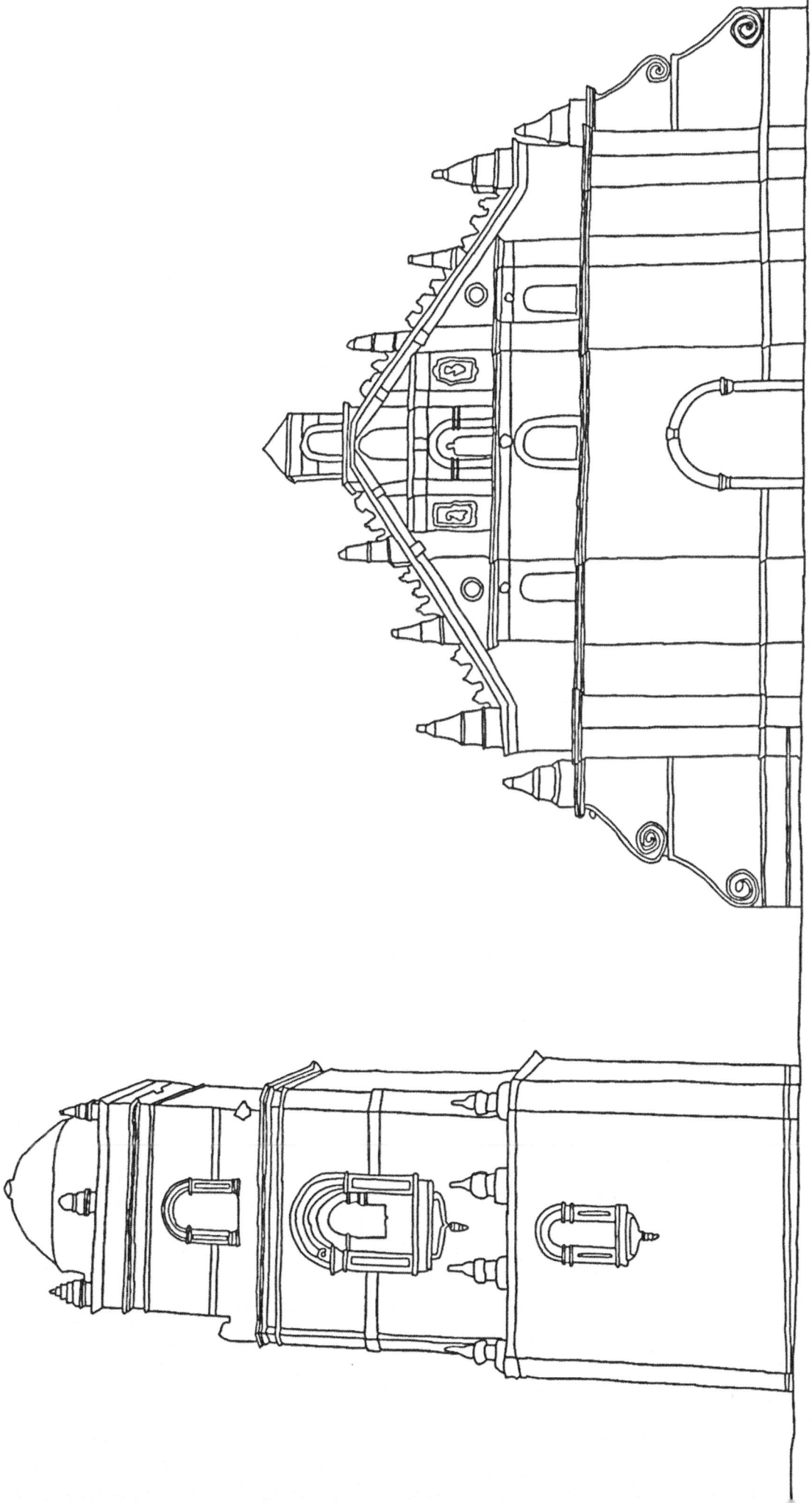

Also known as the Paoay Church, the Church of San Agustin in Ilocos Norte, Philippines, is one of four churches collectively listed in the Baroque Churches of the Philippines World Heritage Site. The church was built in 1710, although work began in 1694.

Gapura Bajang Ratu or the Gate of the Royal Dwarf is a 14th century ornamental gateway in Trowulan, East Java, which was then the capital of the Majapahit Empire. It was probably a ceremonial gate providing access to a noble person's property.

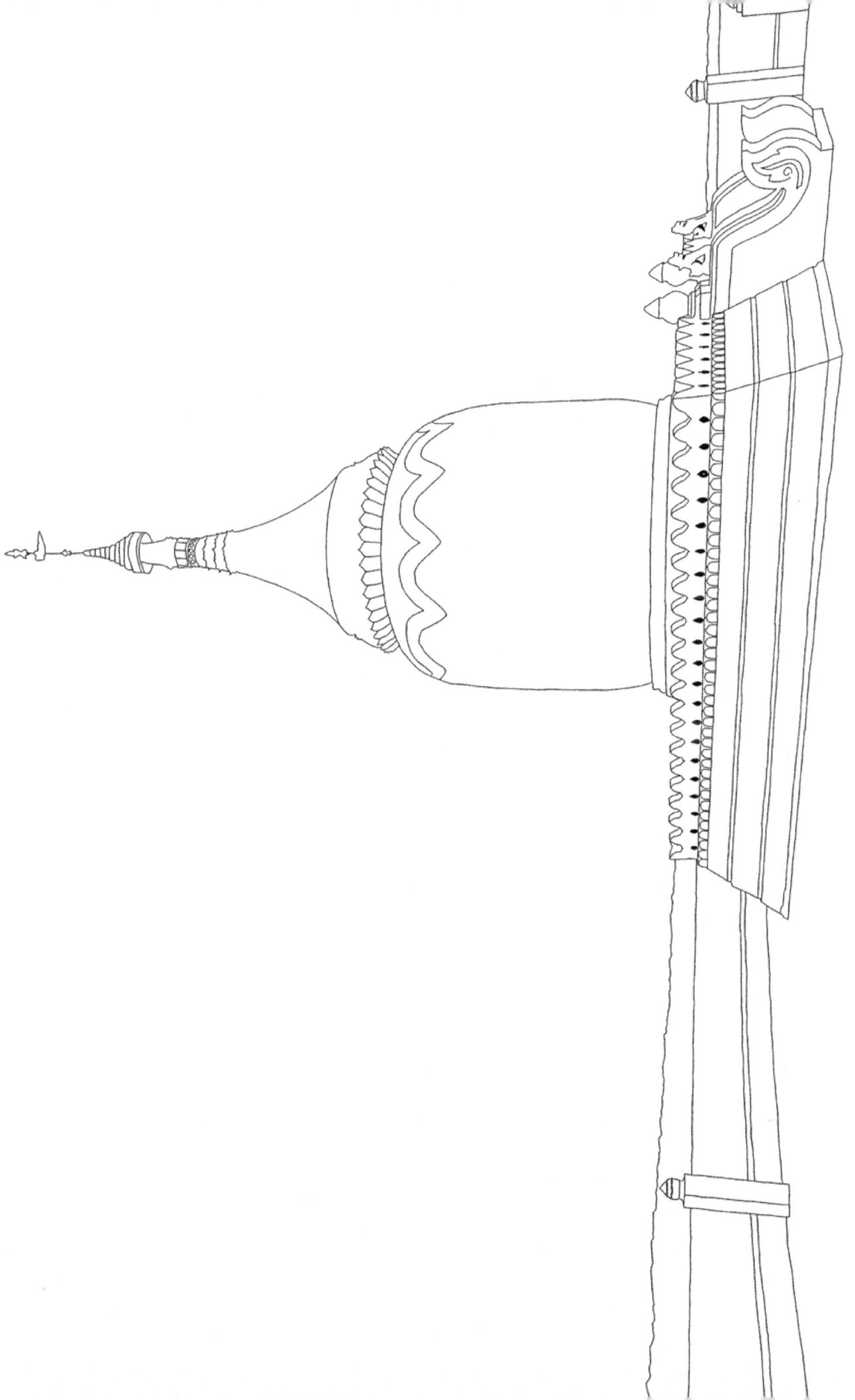

Built at the edge of the Ayeyarwady River in Bagan, Myanmar, the Bupaya pagoda is named after is gourd-like shape ('bu'). It is ascribed to the 2nd or 3rd century CE but was more likely built during the Bagan period (9-11th centuries CE). The original was destroyed by an earthquake in 1975 and has since been reconstructed.

The distinctive red-striped pottery from the Ban Chiang archaeological site in Udon Thani province in Northeast Thailand. Prehistoric people lived in Ban Chiang from around 2,000 BCE but the famous red-painted pottery with the distinctive swirls comes from the later period, between 300 BCE and 200 CE.

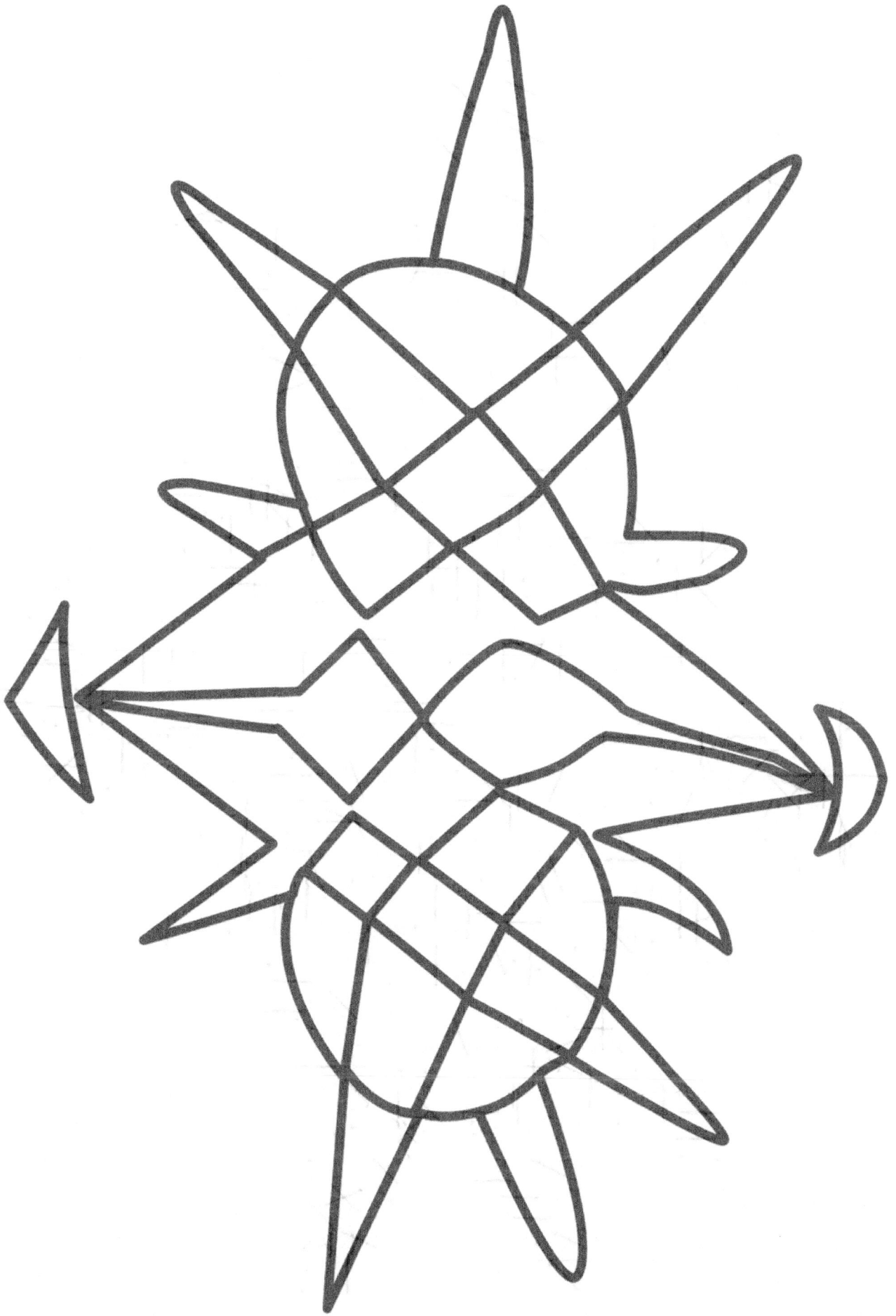

A rock art design from Lene Hara cave in East Timor, located on the eastern end of the island. The age of this paintings is unknown, but archaeological deposits from the cave indicate that it was used by humans some 35,000 years ago.

This bas-relief of a yaksa or nature spirit was found in found in Trà Kiệu in Vietnam's Quảng Nam Province and dated to the 5-6th century CE. It is on display at the Museum of Cham Sculpture in Da Nang.

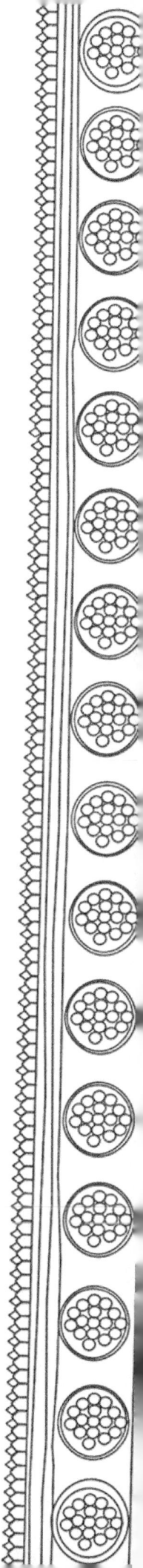

In this bas-relief carving at Angkor Wat, we can see a line of musicians who are accompanying soldiers. The musicians are playing gongs and cymbals and elsewhere in this scene other instruments are depicted. This relief was carved in the 16th century CE, later than the temple's actual construction in the 12th century.

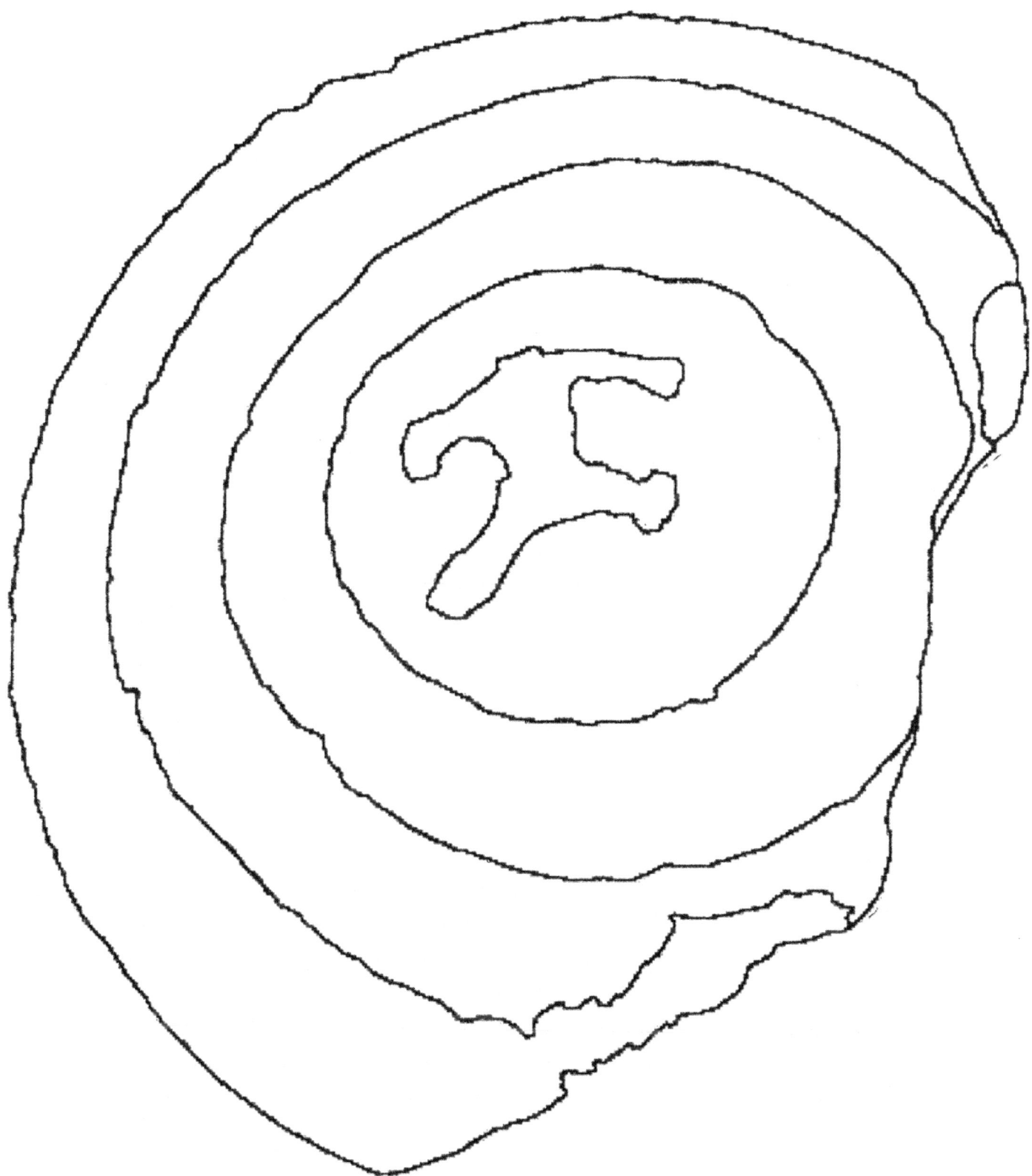

A stone disc with a rare human figure carved on it, from the Plain of Jars (Site 2) World Heritage Site in Laos. Thousands of stone jars and lids can be found across northern Laos, and recent research suggests that the jars may have been placed more than 3,000 years ago.

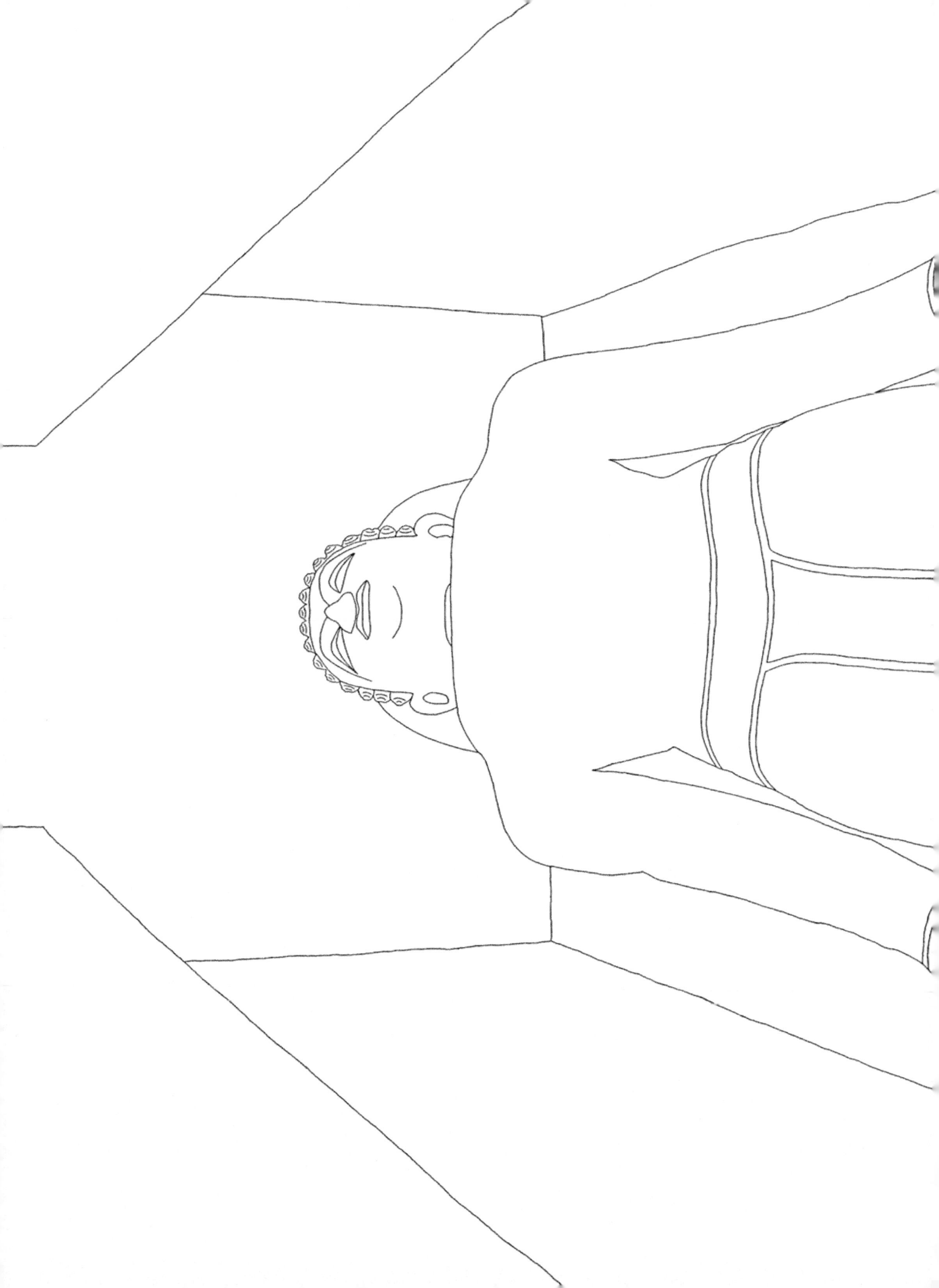

Established in the 13th century, Sukhothai is considered as the beginning of the unified Thai state and its ruins are also a UNESCO World Heritage Site. Wat Maha That or the Temple of the Great Relic is one of the central temples at the Sukhothai Historical Park and probably one of the most visited.

What have these eyes seen over the last 700 years? The face towers of the Bayon in Cambodia was built during the reign of King Jayavarman VII (1125-1218) who is considered one of the greatest rulers of Angkor.

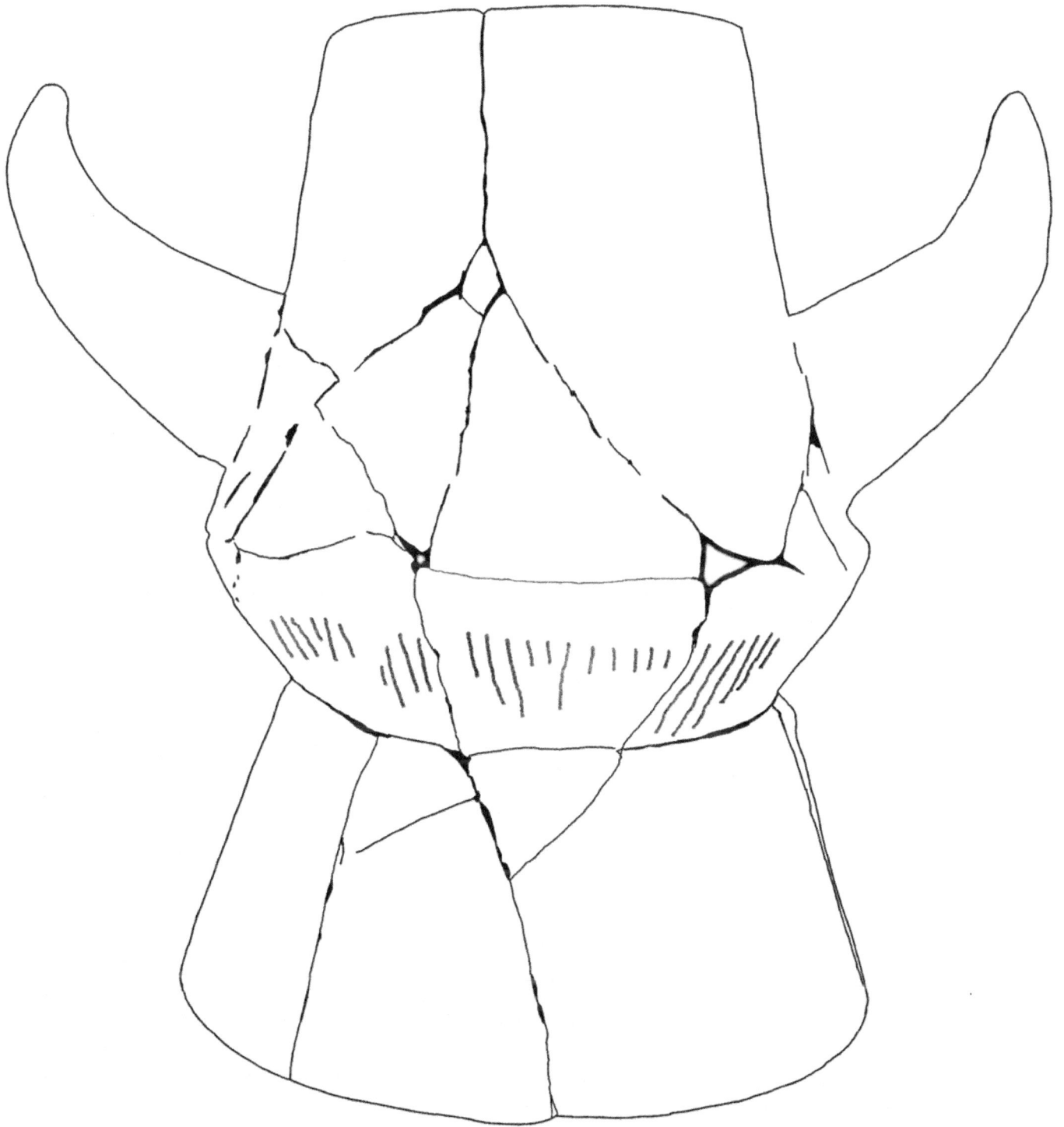

This horned cup is one of the most interesting pieces from the Nong Ratchawat site in Suphan Buri province, Thailand. The site was discovered in 2003, and archaeologists have found numerous burials dating between 3,000-4,000 years ago. The rarity of this vessel may indicate that the person it was buried with was a high-ranking person.

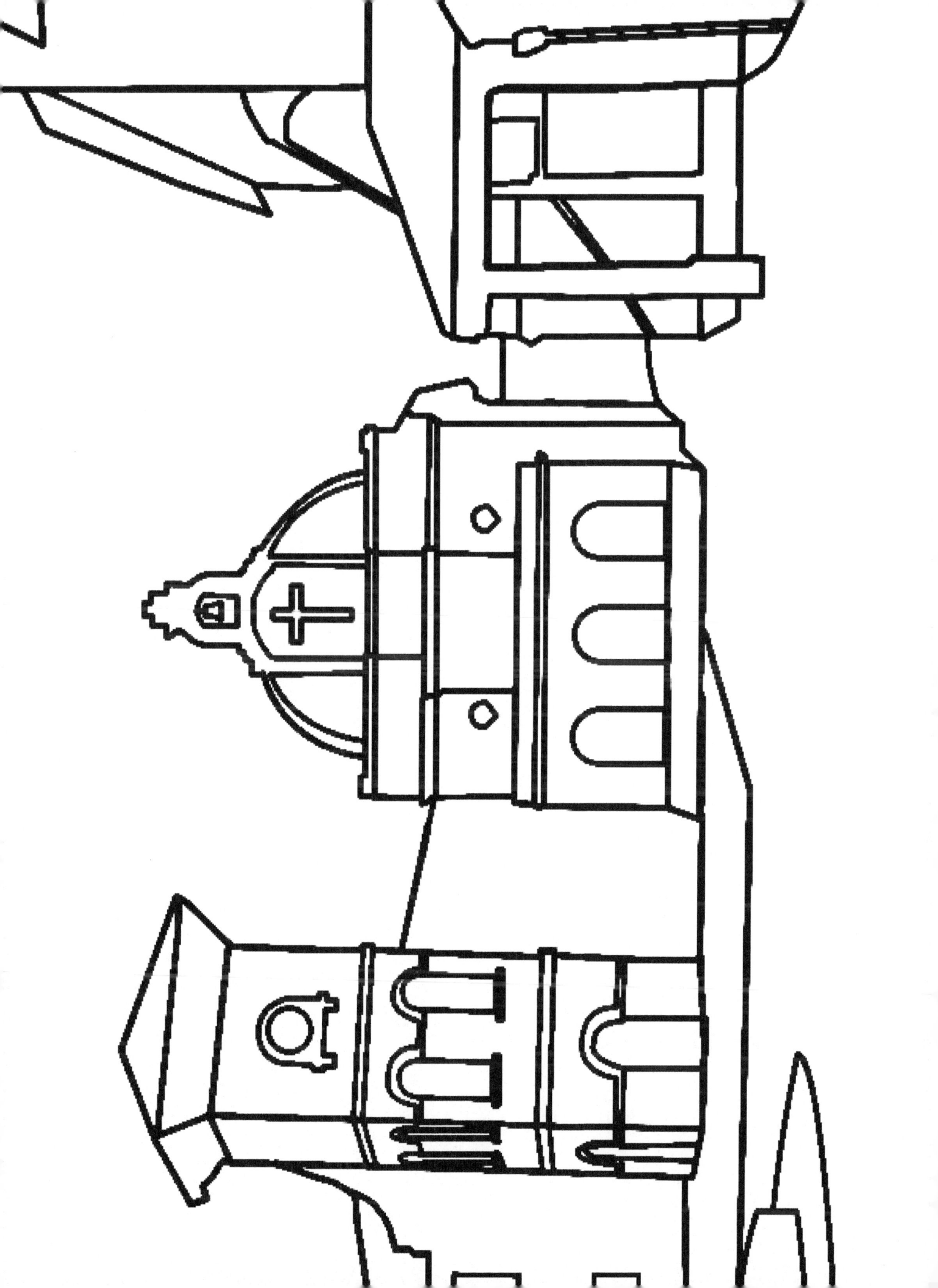

The Stadthuys with its clock tower and the Christ Church are the historic center of Malacca, Malaysia. They were built in the 17th century during the Dutch colonial period. You can't miss them in real life, as they are painted distinctively red. They are now major attractions in this UNESCO World Heritage town.

The Majapahit Rider, so-called because of its Javanese style and approximate 14th-century CE date, was found in the banks of the Singapore River during a 1998 excavation. While headless, other details can be made out such as the saddle which resembles wings, as well as the rider's sarong or loincloth. This figure is made of lead and lead figurines are uncommon in the archaeological record.

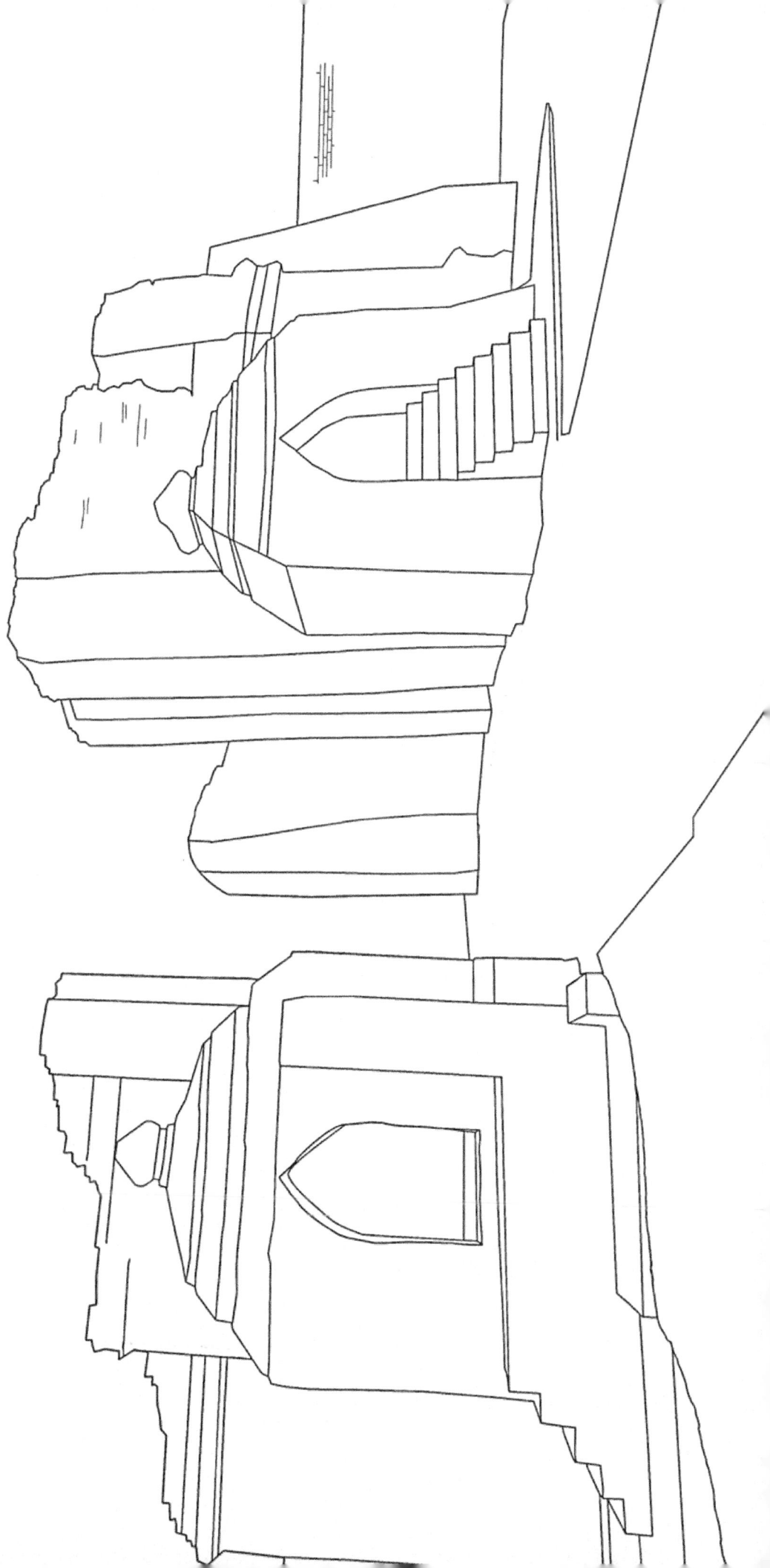

The Tharabha Gate of Old Bagan, Myanmar, is one of the twelve gates to the ancient city and the only one that survives today. You can see this 9th century gate on the eastern side of Old Bagan. The two niches on either side of the entrance are shrines to local spirits or nats.

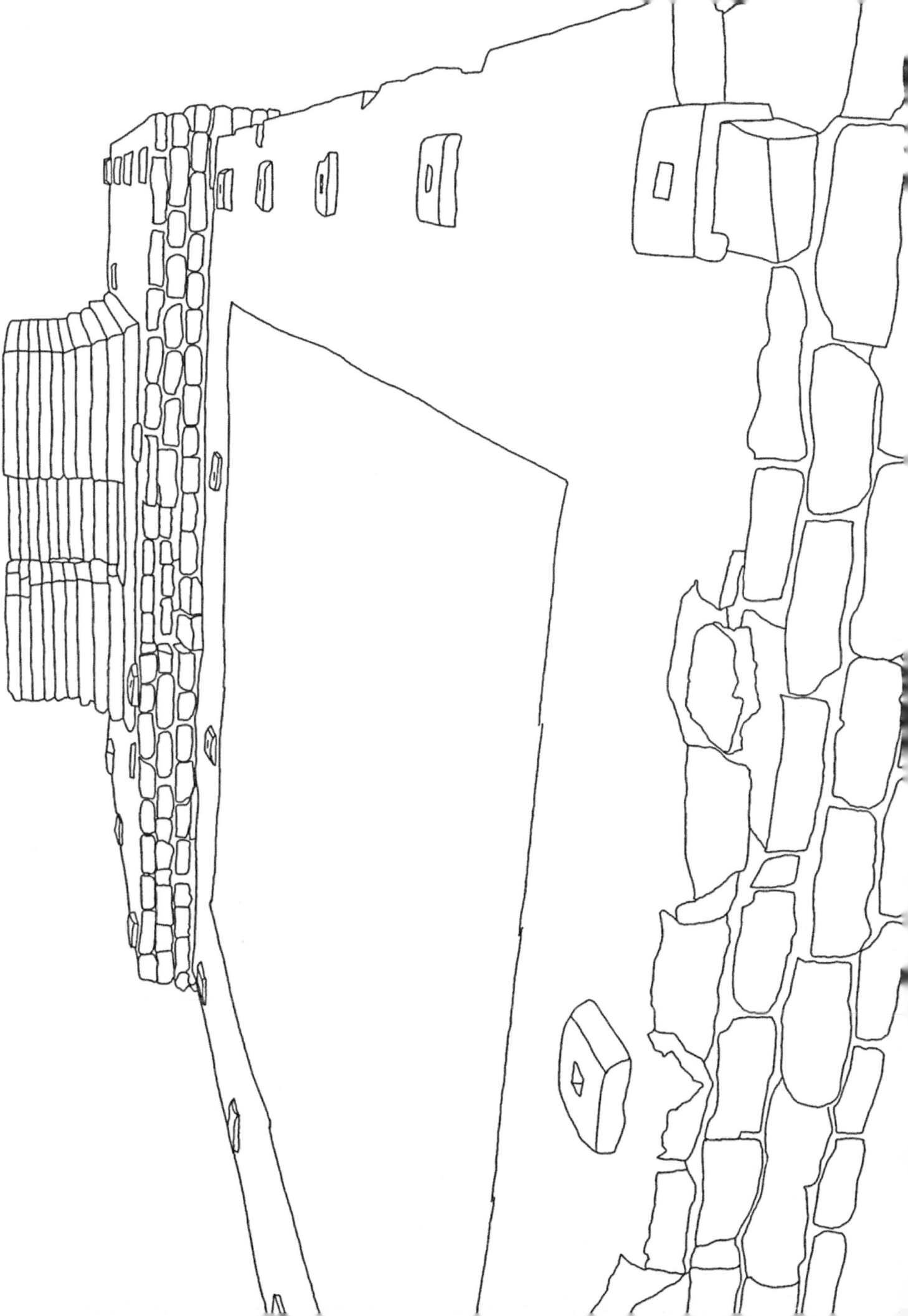

The Bujang Valley of Kedah, Malaysia, contains some pretty cool brick temples dating to the early first millennium of the Common Era. At the Bujang Valley Archaeological Museum, you can see some reconstructions of the temples, but this particular ruin, Candi Batu Pahat, is located in its original place and dated to the 6th century CE.

Can you spot the bird and the fishes? This glazed plate was made in Myanmar around the 15th century CE. The original plate has green and white designs, but you should color it in any way you want!

Another close-up of carved decorations at Cambodia's Angkor Wat. It's easy to think that most ancient temples in Southeast Asia are very symmetrical and can look the same after a while. But when you look at the carvings up close, their minor imperfections remind us that they were all literally hand-crafted.

A final challenge for the more advanced colorists – this is the mouth of the Great Cave at Niah in Sarawak, Malaysia, where the remains of a 45,000-year-old female was found. The Niah Caves are one of the most significant archaeological sites in Borneo and Malaysia.

Printed in Great Britain
by Amazon